3D SNAPSHOTS
BUGS

FOG
CITY
PRESS

Published by Fog City Press,
a division of Weldon Owen Inc.
415 Jackson Street
San Francisco, CA 94111 USA
www.weldonowen.com

WELDON OWEN INC.
President, CEO Terry Newell
VP, Sales and New Business Development Amy Kaneko
VP, Publisher Roger Shaw
Executive Editor Elizabeth Dougherty
Managing Editor, Fog City Press Karen Perez
Editorial Assistant Katharine Moore
Associate Creative Director Kelly Booth
Designer Michel Gadwa
3D Illustration Andy Lackow
Production Director Chris Hemesath
Production Manager Michelle Duggan
Color Manager Teri Bell

Text Sonia Vallabh
Picture Research Brandi Valenza

A WELDON OWEN PRODUCTION
© 2010 Weldon Owen Inc.

ISBN: 978-1-61628-055-0 (Hardcover)
ISBN: 978-1-61628-076-5 (Paperback)

10 9 8 7 6 5 4 3
2014   2013   2012

Printed by RR Donnelley in China

Did you know that more than half of all known creatures are bugs? They may not be very big, but bugs have strength in numbers. They are the most diverse group of animals on Earth!

Whether they're long or short, smooth or spiky, gliding through the air or hiding underground, bugs are everywhere. And that means that anyone can go exploring for bugs... So what are you waiting for?

Not all bugs are
creepy-crawly.
Many are beautiful
and bright.

Some, like these butterflies,
are covered in pretty patterns
and stripes.

Beetles are often
shiny, and come
in all of the colors
of the rainbow.

These bugs all share one thing: polka-dots!

Bright colors can be a warning to other animals. This ladybug's bright red color says that it's not good to eat.

On some bugs, stripes are useful for hiding. On other bugs, bright stripes are a warning to other animals to stay away.

This snail may look slow and harmless, but snails can be bad for the garden because they like to eat the fresh green leaves of our plants.

Bugs come in thousands of wacky shapes and sizes.

Some insects,
like this spiny
flower mantis,
hide by making
themselves look
like something
else: what a
pretty flower this
bug makes!

Other bugs
blend in so well
that they can
hardly be seen!
Can you see the
moth below?

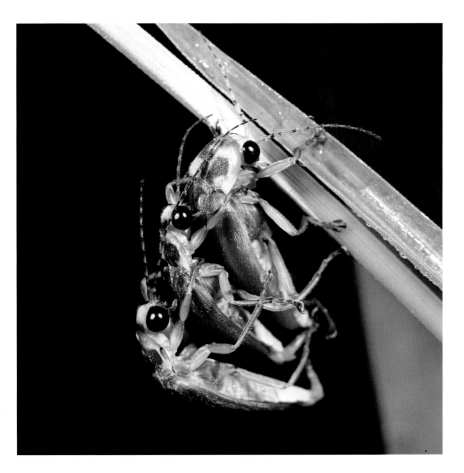

It's easy to see
a busy group
of bugs.

And large bugs
like the stag beetle,
which can be as big
as your hand, are
hard not to notice!

Some bugs have
long snouts for
eating. Others
have big jaws
for fighting.

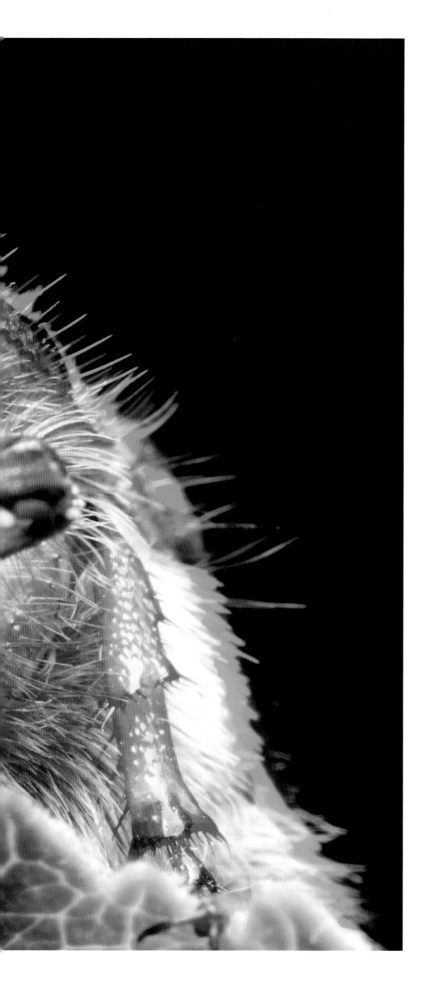

Some insects look
like they have
thick, furry coats!

Many bugs have compound eyes, which is like having thousands of eyes in one. This allows them to see in almost every direction.

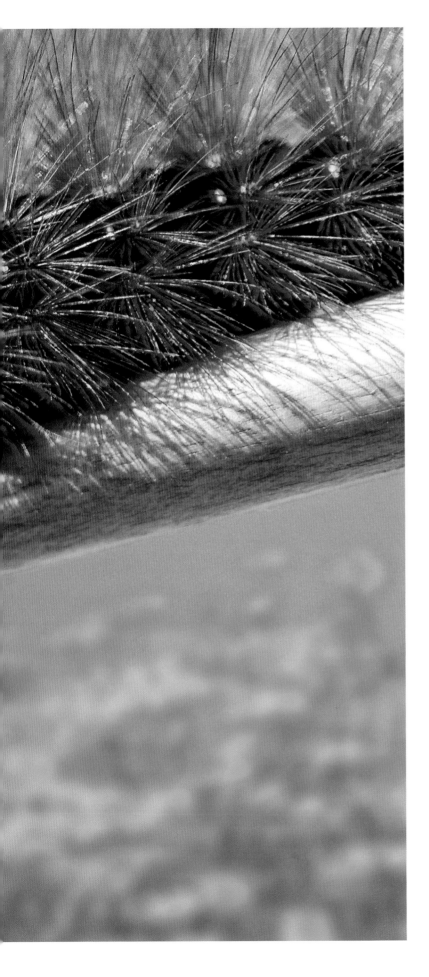

Yellow bear caterpillars cannot see much because their eyes are so small. They must move their front ends back and forth to feel where to go next!

Bugs can change a lot as they grow up. Baby bugs are called larvae or nymphs.

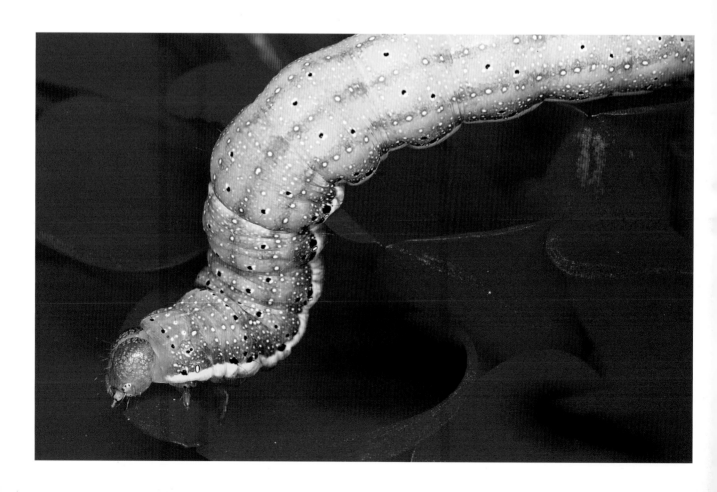

As adults,
bugs may look
completely
different. What
a surprise!

Bugs can often be
found on brightly
colored flowers.

Flowers offer these bugs food, and in return, the bugs spread the flowers' pollen as they move from place to place.

Bugs use their fancy feelers, or antennae, to find the foods that they like to eat.

Caterpillars
spend almost all
day munching
on plants.

Honeybees have a special talent.
They make a food that we like
to harvest and eat—honey! Yum!

This wolf spider looks like it has a different kind of food in mind—probably another bug! Wolf spiders run after their prey.

Other spiders build traps to catch
their dinner unawares.

I wouldn't want to be a little bug when a big bug is hungry.

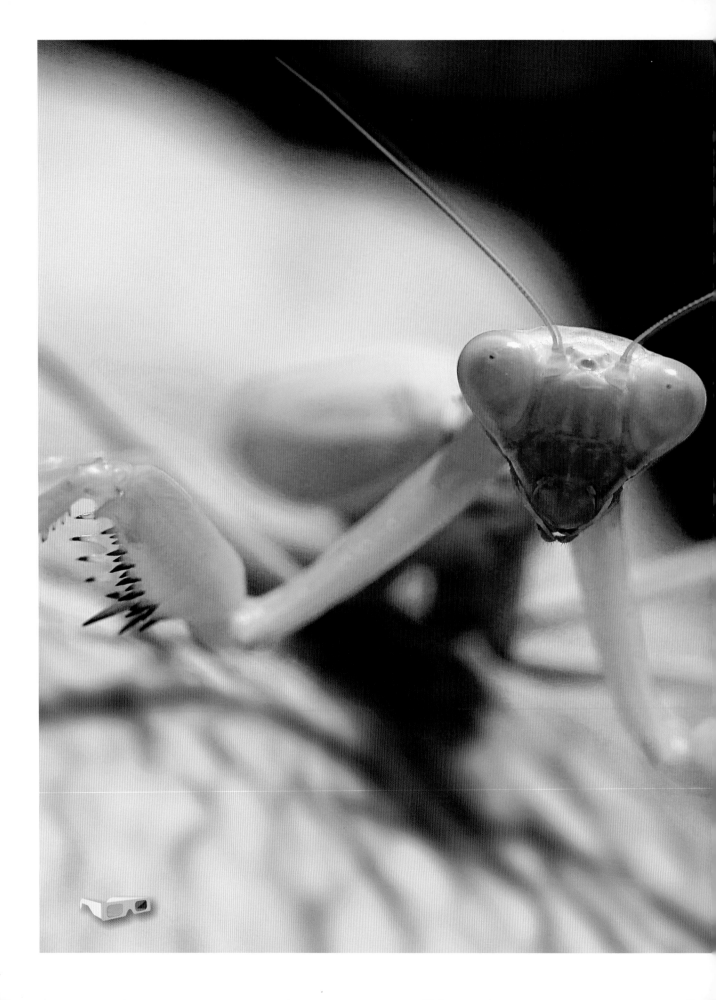

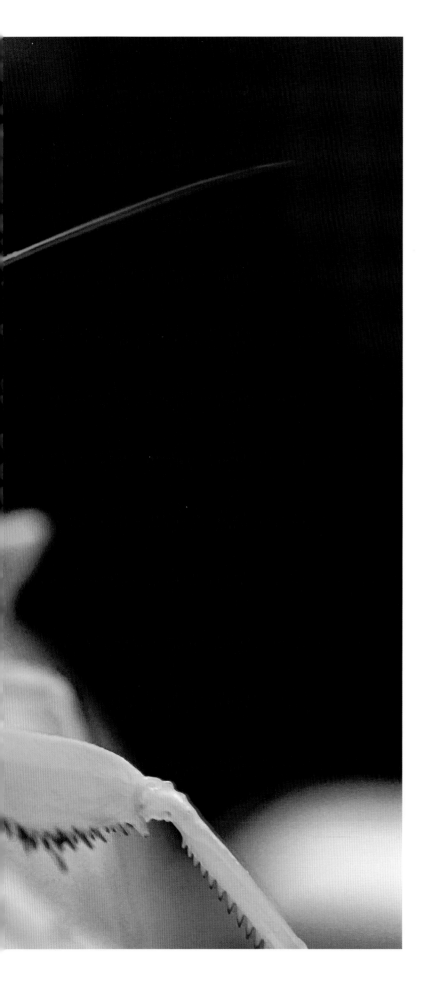

You just never
know who you'll
meet next in the
bug world!

Widow Skimmer Dragonfly

 Ladybug

 Tobacco Hornworm Moth

 Assassin Bug

 Stink Bug

 Jamaican Field Cricket

 Black Swallowtail Butterfly Caterpillar

 Colorado Potato Beetle

 Green June Beetles

 Blue Morpho Butterfly

 Dung Beetle

 Fireflies

 Swallowtail Butterfly

 Garden Snail

 Red Ants

 Butterfly

 Wheel Bug

 Stag Beetle

 Rose Chafer

 Caterpillar

 Long Snout Weevil

 Spotted Cucumber Beetle

 Grasshoppers

 Stag Beetle

 Colorado Beetle Larva

 Spiny Flower Mantis

 Snout Beetle

 Giant Peacock Moth Caterpillar

 Green Shield Bug

 June Beetle

Orb Spider

 Julia Butterfly

 Wolf Spider

 Grasshopper

 Nais Metalmark Butterfly

 Cross Spider

 Yellow Bear Caterpillar

 Bee

 Baboon Spider

 Henry's Marsh Moth Caterpillar

 Ladybug

 Green Shield Bug and Spider

 Beet Armyworm Larva

 Violet Tanbark Beetle

 Banana Spider

 Swallowtail Caterpillar

 Beetle

 Shamrock Spider

 Butterfly

 Swallowtail Caterpillar

 Mantis

 Butterfly

 Honeybees

 Grasshopper

 Common Banner Butterflies

 Bumblebee

ACKNOWLEDGMENTS

Weldon Owen would like to thank the following people for their assistance in the production of this book: Diana Heom, Ashley Martinez, Danielle Parker, Lucie Parker, Phil Paulick, and Erin Zaunbrecher. 3D Conversions by Pinsharp 3D Graphics Liverpool UK.

CREDITS

All images courtesy of Shutterstock.